My Close Encounter with an Extraterrestrial

Dr. Delbert Blair

Second Edition
ISBN 978-0-9961266-8-7

Published by:
    Inner Alchemy's Publishing Inc.
    332 S. Michigan Ave.
    Ste 1032-C141
    Chicago, IL 60604-4434

    info@inneralchemys.com
    www.inneralchemys.com

Printed in the United States of America

Who is Dr. Delbert Blair?

Dr. Delbert Blair is an engineer, research scientist, Metaphysical Teacher and a Historian of the highest level. For over 50 years he has been the director of the Meta Center in Chicago since 1973, a former pastor of his own church and has lectured and answered questions in over 200 forums on various topics like:

- The Facts & Myths about 2012
- The 18th Dynasty of Egypt
- The Face of a Black Woman on the Pyramids of Mars
- Our (2) Suns
- Radiation in Hospitals
- Cells from Hell: The Danger of Cell Phones & Other Energy Vampires
- E.L.F. (Extra Low Frequency) Waves
- Sexual Energy Dangers
- Melanin War's
- Why we should avoid Vaccines
- Return of the Black Cosmic Forces
- Applied Science of Meditation
- What are our E.M.F. Protection products & How it can Help You
- Homosexuality: What it is and What it Ain't

and much, much more….

Dr. Delbert Blair is a very informative presenter and this is why it is not hard to figure out why he was #1 on an unnamed hit list. Dr. Blair has received many death threats; including being poisoned which resulted in his beloved wife's untimely death.

The Great Dr. Delbert Blair has passed away from the physical world on January 31st, 2016. This Great man has awakened hundreds of thousands of people from around the world with his message. And in his memory we can all honor him by rising to our highest vibration internally, and expressing the highest thoughts externally.

During the years many have heard Dr. Delbert Blair do phone conferences with his friend who he refers to as Tony. Dr. Blair and Tony were working on quite a few projects to bring his dream into reality over the years but due to him falling ill only a few of these projects were brought into the light. Tony remains diligent in his love that he has for Dr. Delbert Blair to bring forth various forms of information and sciences that shall change the world forever.

We are happy that many of you in your various ways also help in this journey.

Thank you from the infinity of time and space.

Table of Contents

Chapter 1

Meeting with
Mr. George Adamski

When I met Mr. George Adamski, at a UFO lecture and I was quite elated. How I met him was very interesting which is an understatement. They had a UFO convention I went to and I was in my last year of undergrad school. And when I would go on these trips, nobody would ever go with me because they thought it was a waste of time. So I went there and I was quite taken back because they had some readers (physic) there that were fakes and so on and so forth at the downtown hotel. To make a long story short again, I went there because I was being driven by something I could not at the time explain.

After that time I don't know what I was being driven by, but I know it made a huge imprint in my life. I either wanted to find out were UFOs real or not, I had to know. If they were unreal, I was only going to take one course in life that would have leaded me to heights in academia. If they were real, then it would become more than just an obsession. I wanted to find out more about them and I really didn't know why at the time. So I went downtown Chicago, driven first by a craving for chili and also because George Adamski had arrived.

I had read one of his books called 'Flying Saucers That Landed', and it was something about that book that sparked my interest. I wanted to see what this man actually looked like and I had a multitude of questions that I wanted to ask. When he came to the hotel, I had already caused somewhat a disturbance because I had kind of gone against the director or the one who was putting this thing together. And I asked him, "Why they have all these fakes around?" He says well he had no control of that. He seemed quite a bit perturbed from what I had said he didn't appreciate my belligerence at the time.

When I just crashed into the party that was with George Adamski, they were giving a press interview. And I just came in off from the back of the hotel, wondering why they didn't shoot me or something. But I really didn't know what I was doing; I just know something was driving me. And when I came in there, of course the security came right over to me and there was some of the press and the police present in the auditorium. I was in hearing distance of Mr. Adamski and I said loudly that I wanted to talk to him and that I read one of his books. He told them to let me stay which surprised me too but that shouldn't have surprised me because I must've expected something by coming in there anyway; and he must have known something was to follow.

He was there as the principle speaker and after about 10 minutes he came over to where I was and we talked there on a couch in a hotel for over 6 hours. I told him that I had read his book and that I was very interested in the subject of UFOs. The man had traveled around the world, and talked before Kings and Queens. With all this I said you seem to be sincere, but two things bother me. I said that one; why do you associate yourself with the kinds of people at these fairs, seemingly some of them to be fakes? Also, if this is true what you say, this is probably one of the biggest stories of our century! He stated, well I may be right. I said the second thing is that why is it that some of these things aren't advertised in black neighborhoods as well? He says well it's in downtown Chicago and everyone can come out to it. That there weren't other nationalities present was not his fault. He said well my lecture is tomorrow night, why don't you come back? I said I may not have the funds to do so seeing I scraped up what I could to come here tonight. I'm still in school so I have to make sure I'm able to carry on with that regardless of where this road leads. He said don't worry about it; I'll put your name on my guest list and all you'll have to do is show up at the door and you can get in.

I said ok maybe he will maybe he won't but in the meanwhile I tried to get one of my buddies, tried to get my girlfriend to come with me but none wanted to go to any kind of UFO event. So I came back the next night and when I was there in the audience, the man started doing something that I did not expect him to do and I felt kind of funny because I felt that it was because of our conversation that he did this. He began chastising his audience at the start. Now, he did have about 350 people there. When he got through chastising, he had about 150 people left. It's true. He began to talk about people that were there why was it that if he wasn't saying anything, did they follow him around the world? He talked about the secret government and why did they follow him around? Why did the FBI agents follow him around? And who were these people sitting there with microphones and stuff on? So on and so forth.

People begin to turn red, shutter in their seats obviously a bit uncomfortable about what he was saying. They got up in droves and left and then he swiveled around the seat and then he talked about the various types of psychic readers present. And one woman cursed him when she left the auditorium. When he finished, he lost half of his audience. And then he showed 32 seconds of 16 UFOs in flight flying over an oil refinery and highways where one can resonant with the factual evidence he was showing. He showed quite a bit of one of a kind footage without saying a word and then he finished.

Chapter 2

An moment in time

When he finished it was near the end of the lecture and everybody ran up to the stage, a scene of a mob all trying to ask one man a question if you could envision it. I looked around and I didn't want to take up more of his time because I spent 6 hours with him the day previous. But I looked around for a friendly face when I saw two brothers (Melanated Men aka Black aka Dark in complexion) in the audience. And since the audience was all white (Caucasian) except for them, first thing I thought was okay I can probably speak to them easier. They probably live on the west side or south side of Chicago and they obviously have an interest in UFOs. As I go up to them I noticed that one was a very tall, especially at that time. This was about 1959. He must have been about 6'3. And other guy was fairly short, he must have been about 5'7. One of the things that grabbed my attention about the tall guy was that he was sporting a natural (Natural hair worn on a melanated person, which was allowed to grow), and they weren't wearing naturals at that time. And the other guy had a kind of close crop kind of hair style. When I walked up to them, I said hey brother how are you? He looked over at me at which seemed with contempt then the turned away as I never existed. I said uh-oh. Then the little guy all he did was smile and then he stepped back.

I said dangit, they're trying to pass (trying to act like you are not of that race, class, upbringing, like you're better than another person). Here I go to a UFO convention, see two brothers and they're passing. So I'm looking around for a friendly face again and I see the young lady that was with Mr. Adamski the night before. She was standing over by the doorway to the entrance to the auditorium, so I go over to her, I said the reason I came over here is because I wanted to talk to Mr. Adamski again. I felt I imposed on you guys enough the night before. But I got some more questions especially from this lecture and it seemed no one else wanted to talk to me. She said sure we can talk. I remembered that during the night when the questions were real tough, he looked over at her and she kind of nodded her head. So i noticed he obviously had respect for her. If he respects her than why shouldn't I? Soon as we start our conversation I see her looking passed me. I had my back to the audience and she was facing me. And as she is looking pass me again; I turn around of course to see who she is looking at. And here comes the two brothers that now want to talk that I'm speaking to her.

So these two men come over, and I turn back to her and she starts walking away. Now, I'm getting completely up and out of it, because I try to talk to her, she is moving away and they kind of nodded at each other. So when they come over now, it's not too much they're going to be able to say to me because I got a lot of pride especially in my younger days. So when they came over, they said how are you brother? I said, I'm fine dude but at this time he said I am very sorry. He said I came a long way to see you but I thought one of the people I was supposed to meet was up there with Mr. Adamski. Now, first thing hit me was how can they hear this guy say anything because they were standing back with me when everybody had mobbed up around Mr. Adamski? By the way the whole time this man had not cracked a smile, he had a stern look on his face. The smaller guy constantly smiled. He had an elated face, his eyes just seem to smile at you as he continued to smile. Thus, started a very interesting conversation, he stated that he had traveled a long way to see me because Mr. Adamski said that he should probably come and talk to me.

So I had started asking them the same thing I had asked Adamski to see if they had correlated. And I noticed that this guy went into even more depth. As we were talking I asked one of the questions I had asked him Mr. Adamski which was what is time? I say, you know some of these saucers they say might be time travelers so what is time and how do you interpret this? And he said that time was relative and so on and so forth and continued to talk. He said remember what I told you about time? I said yes. He says well look around you. And that's the first time I thought hey this is going to be a little bit different. I looked around me and there was nobody in the place. When I looked around, there was a man that had a kind of a device that you use to turn bulbs with in the old times and he is going around unscrewing the last two bulbs in this auditorium which looked a lot like the auditorium I was in but I didn't notice these had these funny looking lights in it. The one thing that was taking my mind through a loop was there was no one else around when just a few minutes ago it seems I was standing by the doorway with a 150 people and Mr. Adamski! And now all of a sudden I'm in an empty auditorium with the two brothers and an old guy unscrewing light bulbs? Now he said, let's go on outside and there's no need to lie, I felt kind of funny about doing that.

As I was trying to figure out what went wrong we get out to the elevator and we are just standing there, as one elevator with a load of people were just going down as I'm still looking at these guys. The door opens up and there is a African American woman, small in stature that's driving the elevator. Now bear with because there is significance to all of this. She comes up and opens the elevator door and the first thing little guy does is runs on in, and I saw by the way she looked that she wasn't too ready for this kind of an embrace. But she looked at him with a look that only an African American woman can give. So anyway, we get on the elevator. We go down about 5 flights and we get off on the 1st floor. When we get off on the 1st floor, I went back and I said wait a minute guys can you hold on for a second?! I want to talk to this lady for a minute. So I went back and said hey I just met these guys they've been acting real weird, what happened here and why was he doing this? She says well when they came in when the lecture was about getting ready to start. And they didn't know but I thought because most of the black people were going up to the 6th floor for a jazz and dance event, but they were going to the 5th for for a UFO convention. I assumed they were going upstairs. So when I went the tall guy said we do not want to get off here! And she says weren't you going here? He says certainly not. She says well I reverse the elevator a level down. Well mainly it was Caucasians on the elevator and what the Caucasian made the usual statement. You niggers always sticking together, stuff like this. And when he said that the little guy turned around and looked at him and the man started shaking and drooling. Then he looked at the big guy and the big guy kind of nodded. When they got off the little guy was perturbed and speaking to the big guy in a strange tongue. So, I said to the elevator operator that you mean to tell me they never heard of prejudice before? They never encountered any kind of thing like this?

She said well I don't know but he seemed to be really upset by what the white man said. So I walked back over the brothers that I'm having some strange thoughts about and we started talking and the big guy voice was very powerful. And he was talking loud, so loud in fact I began to feel kind of self-conscious, I said maybe if I get out of the lobby it'll be more comfortable outside. By the way, this was on Dearborn Street about Dearborn and Adam Street. They tore down the hotel now. So we stood outside and there are a lot of people here. We stood out there and I'm still asking him some questions. And one of the questions I ask him is what a Negro is? He says there is no such thing as a Negro; he says the word is necro. I say oh you mean negra. He says it got nothing to do with negra, negra means black. Negro he says were no such thing. He says if you go and look up in your encyclopedia dictionary, you'll find a whole list of words and well later on I did and of course it's necro, necrophil, necrophilia, necrophobic-the dead, the lost, the unknowing, a race unknown, city and places unknown. Plus he says if I wait about 15 minutes he will show me what a necro is. I said boy this is a weird one, glad I don't drink.

Okay, so we're standing there still talking. The little guy kept smiling, saying very little but all he kept saying was "when we're going to eat?" I could have quartered that phrase. This man must have been very hungry. Everything he said was with a smile rather it be hey, hi, when we're going to eat, etc. As we're still talking, the little guy says ohhh wait a minute, when he did that, I said what in the world is that? What he had on his wrist when he pulled his coat up, it was big also understand this was about 1959, it was a big ball of light, it was moving around, and flashing. I said what in the world do you call that? He said it's a chronometer. I said oh yea. I mean you know I left my chronometer at home buddy. It's always pulses like this and as he was explaining what this strange device was, we hear "oh, ho, ho, ha, ha, yea baby, ooohhhh, do that girl...!" I look around the street now this is about 20 min later from when the big guy said I will see what a necro is. Here comes 6 Negros or 'Necros' now coming around the corner. The loudest things you can see from miles, dressed worse than anybody else there, unkempt, and out in the street "yea baby...da...dada dada" I just looked at the man.

I said how did you know that was going to happen 20 minutes ago? He didn't say a word. Little guy, "when we're going to eat?"

I'm going to bring this to a conclusion. I went back and I was saying something again. And that was the first time then, I was beginning to gain respect for something that was a little bit different. Twilight zone stuff, but then, it really begin to hit me and I remember the tears flashed in my eyes. And I jump back like somebody hit me with a lightning bolt because I was thinking thing and the big guy was answering. The more I thought, the more the big guy verbally answered. I said I was thinking that I didn't say that! What the man had been doing for some time was answering questions and queries in my mind and he had done it so smoothly that it wasn't until I was really, I was wrestling with this idea and that's how I noticed. I was thinking it is official, I am definitely outclassed here. I'm definitely out classed here and I maybe I ought to show a bit more respect. At about this time, they had to depart.

Chapter 3

Flight

I was a bit nervous and anxious and at times when I'm like this I tend to make jokes as a cover. So I said I'm going to come with you and we're going to eat aboard your saucer all right?!" He didn't smile and the little guy looked really funny then I said okay well "My name's Delbert and here is my address, Can I get yours?" I think you know the answer to that one. I said well, will I see either of you again? He said you will see him (The little guy) but you won't see me. He said I came along way to see you. This was something special because of the things that you may do. So I asked him of course where can I get more information. He said you could go to a metaphysical bookstore. I asked what was a metaphysical bookstore? He said you'll see. I said thank you. These are the wonderful answers I got! I asked him do UFOs actually exist? He said, well why don't you just watch the skies for the next week. I said well, I have been watching the skies for the last few years and nothing happened why not watch for next week. And then we parted ways.

During the next week, I was watching the skies during the day and most, In fact, I often said one of these nights I am going to get hit in the head looking up. I was coming home as usual, alone at about 10:30 at night and I was looking up and I kept thinking about the meeting. And I think it was about the third day after it. Then I see 3 stars begin to move and of course, when you see something like that. You say uh-oh now, nah, I didn't see it. And then they seemed to move really quick then stopped and then they began to move again. They started to come down, toward me fairly fast and they were coming down in formation. When they got to what appeared to be more than 500 feet above the building, I couldn't hear a sound as you would with typical air craft. I couldn't hear anything. They leveled off and came straight across. But where I was located to get to my apartment house, it would have taken me about 20 more feet and I lived on the second floor. I had to go up. Open the door. Run through the house. I lived in a place where they called it the quadrangle. And it was big square out in the back.

As I stood there looking up into the sky the UFO's revolved and then slowly went out for 20 minutes straight east going out over Lake Michigan. There are some things that happened after that i will not bore you with and they're kind of personal which was not the end my contacts and sittings but that verifies for me that there were UFO's because I saw them with my very own eyes.

I want to now share with you something that very few people have seen. These are very good photographs taken over Switzerland and here is one over the mountains of Switzerland (Dr. Blair speaking to audience at an event where this was recorded)? Here is one over a couple of twin peaks. Here is one showing, landing down on terrain. You can see some of the houses here again in Switzerland and you see the same thing on the other side, this one and this one. You get excellent trajectory. You get excellent background, easy to state whether they're fakes or not. Can you see them? Here is one that's classified. It shows a French mirage jet fighter chasing one. What happened was as this French mirage jet fighter comes close to it, this thing just simply disappears and it disappears miles away. But from this perspective you can get the whole view. This is a blow up on your left and the actual photograph on your right. I want to show you this last one if I can find it. I don't want to take up too much of your time. Oh, here's one that came in camera view so it can be photographed and stood there and you can see the actual camera that took it.

Conclusion simply is this, UFOs are real. It is not just one type but are many and some that you see don't come from outer-space but from the earth itself, the inner earth. Where the real rulers of earth live and have for some time and are about to make their presence known to man again. They came out when man entered into the nuclear age. Before that time there have been certain tribes and people who still held psychic ability and spirituality. Do not fight your psychic ability if it's beginning to be brought back to you folks. It is your cosmic consciousness and we've gotten so westernized now that we don't even want to get back what took thousands of years to develop. It is a gift that many people fought for thousands of years to retain.

For anyone watching and listening from the present day or in the future recordings, I wish you well and Creator Bless.